The Challenger

by
Timothy Levi Biel

LUCENT
B·O·O·K·S

These and other titles are available in the Lucent World Disasters Series:

The Armenian Earthquake	**The Ethiopian Famine**
The Bhopal Chemical Leak	**The Hindenburg**
The Black Death	**Hiroshima**
The Challenger	**The Irish Potato Famine**
Chernobyl	**Krakatoa**
The Chicago Fire	**Pompeii**
The Crash of 1929	**The San Francisco Earthquake**
The Dust Bowl	**The Titanic**

Library of Congress Cataloging-in-Publication Data

Biel, Timothy L.
    The Challenger / by Timothy Levi Biel ; illustrations by Brian McGovern.
        p. cm. — (World disasters)
    Summary: Examines the Challenger disaster from a scientific and
historic perspective and discusses its effect on the space shuttle program.
    Includes bibliographical references.
    ISBN 1-56006-013-1
    1. Challenger (Spacecraft)—Accidents—Juvenile literature.
[1. Challenger (Spacecraft) 2. Space shuttles. 3. Astronautics—
Accidents.] I. McGovern, Brian, ill. II. Title. III. Series.
TL793.B494 1990
363.12'4—dc20   90-6255
                                                                          CIP

To Marko and Opal Rubich

Table of Contents

Preface
The World Disasters Series

World disasters have always aroused human curiosity. Whenever news of tragedy spreads, we want to learn more about it. We wonder how and why the disaster happened, how people reacted, and whether we might have acted differently. To be sure, disaster evokes a wide range of responses—fear, sorrow, despair, generosity, even hope. Yet from every great disaster, one remarkable truth always seems to emerge: in spite of death, pain, and destruction, the human spirit triumphs.

History is full of disasters, arising from a variety of causes. Earthquakes, floods, volcanic eruptions, and other natural events often produce widespread destruction. Just as often, however, people accidentally bring suffering and distress on themselves and other human beings. And many disasters have sinister causes, like human greed, envy, or prejudice.

The disasters included in this series have been chosen not only for their dramatic qualities, but also for their educational value. The reader will learn about the causes and effects of the greatest disasters in history. Technical concepts and interesting anecdotes are explained and illustrated in inset boxes.

But disasters should not be viewed in isolation. To enrich the reader's understanding, these books present historical information about the time period, and interesting facts about the culture in which each disaster occurred. Finally, they teach valuable lessons about human nature. More acts of bravery, cowardice, intelligence, and foolishness are compressed into the few days of a disaster than most people experience in a lifetime.

Dramatic illustrations and evocative narrative lure the reader to distant cities and times gone by. Readers witness the awesome power of an exploding volcano, the magnitude of a violent earthquake, and the hopelessness of passengers on a mighty ship passing to its watery grave. By reliving the events, the reader will see how disaster affects the lives of real people and will gain a deeper understanding of their sorrow, their pain, their courage, and their hope.

Introduction

Cape Canaveral: January 28, 1986

Early Tuesday morning, the sunlight began to filter through the dark, crisp air over the Kennedy Space Center at Cape Canaveral, Florida. Poised in an upright position on the launchpad was the space shuttle *Challenger.*

Many reporters and onlookers had come to see the launch of Flight 51-L because it carried Sharon Christa McAuliffe, who was about to become the United States' first private citizen in space. As the winner of President Ronald Reagan's Teacher in Space program, McAuliffe and her sparkling personality had stirred more public enthusiasm for the space program than Americans had seen since the first moon landing in 1969.

Something else was unusual about this morning in northern Florida: it was uncommonly cold. The night before, the temperature had dropped to twenty-three degrees Fahrenheit. Icicles hung from the launchpad and sparkled in the sunlight.

The sun began to warm the frigid air and melt the icicles on the launchpad. Still, it remained the

The Challenger's Place in History

1500
Leonardo da Vinci sketches plans for a flying machine

1783
Joseph and Etienne Montgolfier of France invent the hot-air balloon

1854
Sir George Cayley, the "Father of Aerodynamics," conducts a successful glider flight

1903
The Wright brothers achieve controlled, motorized flight at Kitty Hawk

1914
World War I begins; airplanes used for reconnaisance, then for bombing enemy targets

1927
Charles Lindbergh flies the *Spirit of St. Louis* solo from New York to Paris in 33.5 hours

1932
Amelia Earhart flies from Newfoundland to Ireland. Later in the year she flies solo across the United States

1941
First jet aircraft developed

1945
The B-29 Superfortress *Enola Gay* brings an end to the war by dropping an atomic bomb on Hiroshima, Japan

1947
United States Air Force is created; Chuck Yeager breaks the sound barrier in *X-1*

1957
USSR launches first earth-orbiting satellite, *Sputnik I*

1961
Soviet cosmonaut Yuri Gagarin is the first person to orbit the earth; Alan B. Shepard Jr. makes the first American suborbital spaceflight

1962
John Glenn is the first American to orbit the earth

coldest day on which a shuttle launch had ever been attempted. The mission management team at Kennedy had been monitoring the weather throughout the night. Twice that morning they had ordered reports from a special ice inspection team. Twice, they had decided it was safe to launch.

At 10:35 A.M., thirty minutes before the scheduled launch, two women and five men wearing lightweight, powder blue jumpsuits stepped out of a shiny silver van and strode jubilantly toward the launch-pad. This was the crew of the *Challenger*. Their eagerness to get the launch underway showed. "It's a great day for a launch," remarked the crew's commander, Dick Scobee.

As the crew boarded the elevator that took them to the *Challenger's* flight deck, it did seem like a great day for a launch. Inside the Launch Control Building, the mission management team went through a final checklist of potential hazards, from weather conditions to mechanical problems, then gave their final order: "All systems go!" Everyone on this team was confident that the launch would be perfect.

Yet just before the launch, in one or two offices at the Kennedy Space Center and a few more offices in Brigham City, Utah, a handful of people watched their TV sets nervously, expecting the worst and hoping they were wrong. What did these few people know and fear that would soon shock the entire world? Why didn't they stop the launch and save the lives of the seven astronauts on board the *Challenger*? Their story is the key in explaining the *Challenger* disaster, and it is a story that begins several years before the design for the *Challenger* was ever drawn.

1963
Soviet astronaut Valentina Tereshkova is the first woman in space

1965
Soviet astronaut Aleksei Leonov takes the first "space walk"

1967
Virgil Grissom, Edward White, and Roger Chaffee die in *Apollo 1* fire during ground tests

1968
First U.S. moon mission, *Apollo 8*

1969
Apollo 11's Neil Armstrong is the first person to walk on the moon

1971
Soyuz 11's three cosmonauts die during reentry when craft loses pressurization

1973
First American orbiting space station, *Skylab,* is launched

1975
U.S.-U.S.S.R. joint space flight

1981
First U.S. space shuttle, *Columbia,* launched

1984
Crew of *Salyut 7* sets space endurance record: 237 days

1986
The *Challenger* explodes seventy-three seconds into its mission, killing all seven crew members aboard

1989
Space probe *Voyager 2* transmits pictures of Neptune back to earth

1990
Hubble Space Telescope launched into orbit around earth

One

A Heroic Tradition

Even though no American has ever died in space, astronauts have always known the dangers of space travel. That is one reason manned space exploration has been controversial in the United States.

Since its infancy, many astronomers, physicists, and other scientists have believed that space exploration could proceed faster, more effectively, and less expensively if people were not put in space. The features and facilities for keeping humans safe and healthy in space require additional time and money to develop. These scientists argue that an unmanned spacecraft could be controlled just as well as a manned craft and could gather just as much information. Nevertheless, manned space flight has always been a goal of the U.S. space program, which began over thirty years ago.

On April 12, 1961, Yuri Gagarin of the Soviet Union became the first human in space. This event sent a shock wave through the American public who believed that this accomplishment proved the United States was seriously behind the Soviet Union in space exploration. President John F. Kennedy reacted aggressively, arguing that the United States could not tolerate second place. Since then, much of the U.S. space program has been conducted as a race to catch up with and surpass the Soviets.

Only a month later, the United States launched its first astronaut, Alan Shepard, into space. Unlike Gagarin, however, Shepard did not orbit the earth. He flew about one hundred miles above the earth's surface and returned to earth. The Soviets still appeared to be ahead in the space race, but President Kennedy pushed for more funding and faster development of the manned space program. He decided that the American people needed an attainable goal, something they could set their sights on. Kennedy decided on an ambitious plan—to land astronauts on the moon.

Kennedy requested a report from the National Aeronautics and Space Administration (NASA) estimating how soon it could land humans on the moon. NASA concluded that with appropriate funding, it could achieve that goal before the end of the decade (by 1970). The landing would be expensive, but the NASA

The *Apollo II* lunar module as it ascends from the moon to rendezvous with the main spacecraft. The earth is in the background. The *Apollo* moon missions were among the most successful ever attempted.

report expressed the belief that the rewards would justify the cost:

> It is our belief that manned exploration to the surface of the moon represents a major area in which international competition in space will be conducted. The orbiting of machines is not the same as orbiting or landing of man. It is man in space that captures the imagination of the world.

President Kennedy was convinced, and on May 25, just three weeks after Alan Shepard's historic foray into space, Kennedy made this bold announcement:

> I believe that this nation should commit itself to achieving the goal, before the decade is out, of landing a man on the moon and returning him safely to the earth. No single space project in this period will be more impressive to mankind or more important for the long-range exploration of space, and none will be so difficult or expensive to accomplish.

The goal of sending a person to the moon became known as Project Apollo, and to this day it remains the single most expensive space project in history. It required entirely new technologies, including building rockets far more powerful than anything either the United States or the Soviet Union had ever built. In their excitement over the Apollo project, Kennedy and NASA representatives rarely discussed the scientific advantages of a manned lunar landing over an unmanned landing. Instead, they stressed that such a project would "capture the imagination of the world."

One of the first requirements for reaching this goal was building a rocket powerful enough to escape the earth's gravity. In 1962, NASA used a powerful new rocket, called the Saturn, to launch an unmanned spacecraft into orbit about 163 miles above the earth. On February 20 of that year, John Glenn became the first American to orbit the earth. America's space program was in high gear. NASA was well-funded, and the romance and challenge of space travel—and of beating the Soviets to the moon—became a national goal.

Beat the Soviets to the Moon

After Kennedy was assassinated in 1963, Lyndon Johnson became president. He was just as determined as Kennedy to beat the Soviet Union to the moon. By the end of 1963, the United States had flown twelve manned space flights. Each was part of the Mercury program, which placed small, one-person space capsules into orbit for progressively longer periods. During the final Mercury flight, in May 1963, astronaut Gordon Cooper orbited the earth for thirty-four hours.

The following year, scientists, engineers, and astronauts were busy preparing for the next phase of the manned exploration of space: the Gemini program.

As its name suggests, this program entailed building and flying space capsules big enough for two astronauts. The Gemini capsules were not only bigger than the Mercury capsules had been but they were more sophisticated. The astronauts could steer and maneuver these capsules so that they could switch their orbit levels. This kind of maneuverability and control would be needed for a moon landing.

In the second manned Gemini flight, launched June 3, 1965, astronaut Ed White became the first American to leave his spacecraft and walk in space. With each successive flight, American astronauts became better adapted to the conditions of space, both inside and outside the protective environment of their space capsules.

In December 1965, *Gemini 7,* with Frank Borman and James Lovell aboard, set an American endurance record by staying in orbit

WHAT IS ORBIT SPEED?

To stay in orbit, an object has to reach an exact speed that will precisely balance it against the force of gravity. At this speed, the object is moving fast enough to keep gravity from pulling it to earth. And gravity is strong enough to keep the object from flying off into space. As long as its speed does not change, the object will continue to orbit the earth. The instant it exceeds orbit speed, however, the object will fly out into space. And the moment it drops below orbit speed, it will begin to fall toward the earth.

Orbit speed varies according to altitude. For example, orbit speed at an altitude of two hundred miles above the earth is about seventeen thousand miles per hour. But at higher altitudes the force of gravity is weaker, so objects do not have to travel as fast to overcome it. At an altitude of two thousand miles, orbit speed is only sixty-nine hundred miles per hour. Pictured below is the *Skylab* space station in orbit above the earth.

11

for two full weeks. This proved that humans could live and work in space for at least two weeks with no harmful effects. The *Gemini 7* also broke new ground when its launch had been timed so that it would meet another space capsule in orbit, the unmanned *Gemini 6*. James Lovell then piloted the *Gemini 7* capsule so that it came within a few feet of the unmanned capsule.

In later flights of the Gemini program, astronauts perfected the method of fully docking, or linking together, two spacecraft in space. This technique would be critical in a moon landing in which the large ship sent to the moon would not actually land. Instead, a smaller lunar landing craft would land and later launch itself back to the orbiting "mother ship."

Following these successes, NASA embarked with confidence on its Apollo project in 1967. The goal was to place a person safely on the moon before 1970. Just as the project was getting underway, however, the U.S. space program experienced its first tragedy. On January 27, 1967, during a test exercise on the ground, the *Apollo 1* space capsule caught fire. Trapped inside, astronauts Gus Grissom, Edward White, and Roger Chaffee died less than one minute after the fire began.

The tragedy took Americans by surprise. As a result, the first serious challenges to manned space projects were voiced in Congress and on the street. Critics of manned space expeditions had pointed out that all the safety features and facilities for human survival in space made the Apollo project cost about

An illustration depicts the linking of two spacecraft in space. Pictured here are the Soviet *Soyuz* spacecraft and the U.S. *Apollo* spacecraft.

ten times more than an unmanned program would have cost. And it still was not safe.

Leaders Lost Interest

With the deaths of Grissom, White, and Chaffee, the number of critics grew. The fact that this was also a time of change and turmoil in American society in general added to NASA's troubles. The late 1960s were marked by assassinations, race riots, and protests against the Vietnam War. Patriotism and faith in the U.S. government were eroding. Many Americans, including congressional leaders, lost interest in the space program. With issues such as poverty, civil rights, and the war in Southeast Asia demanding their attention, few legislators championed the space program. As a result, in 1968, NASA experienced its first budget cut.

With this setback, NASA did not launch the first Apollo capsule until October 1968. The success of this flight prompted President Johnson to make a bold proposal. He urged NASA to attempt a manned orbit of the moon before the end of 1968.

At President Johnson's urging, on December 21, 1968, *Apollo 8* was launched toward the moon. In a live television broadcast from space on Christmas Eve, Frank Borman, one of the three astronauts aboard *Apollo 8*, read the story of Jesus' birth from the Bible as the *Apollo 8* capsule circled the moon. It was one of the most memorable and stirring moments in the story of manned space flight.

Apollo 8 helped put the space program back in high gear. The moment for launching *Apollo 11*, the historic flight to the moon, came on July 16, 1969. Astronauts Neil Armstrong, Edwin "Buzz" Aldrin, and Michael Collins boarded the spacecraft. Millions of Americans watched on their TV sets as a huge Saturn 5 booster rocket launched *Apollo 11* on its way.

On July 20, 1969, five months before John F. Kennedy's deadline, Michael Collins guided the command craft into its orbit only ten miles above the moon's surface. Then Armstrong and Aldrin boarded the lunar lander (known as the *Eagle*) and began their descent to the moon. At 4:17 P.M., eastern daylight time (EDT), the landing module touched down. A few hours later, TV cameras mounted on the *Eagle* transmitted live to viewers around the world pictures of Neil Armstrong walking down the ladder from the *Eagle* toward the moon's barren, dusty surface. Looking like an alien creature in his space suit, Armstrong paused briefly on the bottom rung. It was precisely 10:56 P.M., EDT. At that moment, he hopped off the ladder and became the first human to set foot on the moon. As he did, he made his famous statement, "That's one small step for a man, one giant leap for mankind."

Astronaut Neil Armstrong during his historic walk on the moon.

Buzz Aldrin soon followed Armstrong down the ladder, and for two hours the astronauts explored and collected rocks and ground samples. Before returning to their craft, they planted an American flag and spoke by radio with President Richard Nixon in the White House. Nixon emphasized the importance of this accomplishment:

> For every American, this has to be the proudest day of our lives. For one priceless moment in the whole history of man, all the people on this earth are truly one.

After the first Apollo moon landing, a strange thing began to happen to the U.S. space program. The race to the moon was over. As soon as the United States had beaten the Soviets to the moon, many Americans lost interest in space exploration. Even the press treated later Apollo flights to the moon as little more than technical publicity stunts. And the flights were so perfectly executed that they had none of the daring drama of earlier space missions. Finally, many Americans began to wonder whether the race to the moon had really been worthwhile. Except for a couple thousand pounds of moon rocks, critics recognized few visible rewards from the great cost and effort of sending humans to the moon.

The space program had reached

a critical turning point. There was great disagreement within the scientific community and among political leaders about what the next goal for the space program should be.

Shortly after the last Apollo mission, in an attempt to renew public interest in space, NASA proposed sending humans to Mars by the year 1990.

In pursuit of this goal, NASA tested the idea of an orbiting space station by building and launching a small, temporary one called *Skylab* in 1973. *Skylab* remained in orbit for three years, from 1973 through 1975. It contained laboratory facilities and living quarters. This allowed astronauts to stay at the space station and work up to two or three months at a time. Astronauts flew to *Skylab* aboard Apollo-style space capsules.

Transport System (STS), or shuttle program. This program was supposed to accomplish several goals. The shuttle could be used to conduct experiments in space or observe astronomical phenomena. It could also be used as a platform from which to launch satellites or experimental space-based weapons.

Shuttle Is Reusable

But the main reason Congress supported the shuttle was that it was reusable. In fact, NASA presented a plan to Congress for a fleet of reusable space vehicles that would be practical and self-supporting within ten years. These vehicles would be launched into orbit like rockets and would return to land on earth like airplanes.

NASA predicted that the shuttle could launch communication satellites, weather satellites, and planetary observatories in space for private companies. These companies would pay NASA for the use of the shuttle, thus paying for the program. To achieve these goals, NASA proposed a fleet of six or seven shuttles.

At times, the challenges of building this complex vehicle seemed insurmountable. Never before had a spacecraft been designed to be reusable after leaving and reentering the earth's atmosphere. At the point of reentry, while moving at supersonic speeds, the surface temperature of the shuttle would heat up to more than twenty-seven hundred degrees Fahrenheit. To withstand

Two

A Race Against Time

As the 1970s progressed, the voices of protest against manned space flights grew stronger. Civil rights, the energy crisis, and the Vietnam War all continued to distract Americans' attention. In 1974, U.S. troops withdrew in defeat from Vietnam. President Richard Nixon resigned as a result of the Watergate scandal. Pride and trust in national leaders dropped to an all-time low.

These national tragedies also affected NASA. It had few strong supporters in Congress, which cut NASA's budget drastically. NASA was forced to put on hold both the permanent space station and the voyage to Mars. In fact, the only manned project to survive the congressional budget ax was the Space

The *Challenger* space shuttle before takeoff.

such temperatures, the entire shuttle had to be covered with tiles that were lightweight yet capable of resisting the scorching heat. Reusable rocket engines were another new challenge. Each of the shuttle's three main engines had to deliver about seventy-seven thousand horsepower. They had to be small enough to fit inside the tail end of the shuttle yet durable enough to be reused fifty or sixty times.

Ready for Launch

Finally, on April 12, 1981, nearly two years behind schedule, the shuttle prototype *Columbia* stood ready for launch at the Kennedy Space Center. It carried two crew members, Bob Crippen and John Young. It was twenty years to the day since Yuri Gagarin had become the first human being in space. As the countdown reached zero, the tall, slender SRBs straddling the *Columbia* roared to life. Their blinding flames turned the clear Florida sky bright orange as they lifted the *Columbia* and its huge external fuel tank skyward. Sixty miles above the earth, the SRBs detached from the shuttle according to plan and floated beneath their parachutes back to earth. Powered now only by its own three main engines, the shuttle reached a speed of about seventeen thousand miles per hour as it soared toward its orbit height about three hundred miles above the earth's surface.

From the moment of its launch to its return two days later at Edwards

The space shuttle *Columbia* awaits takeoff.

LAUNCHING, ORBITING, AND LANDING

The space shuttle's launch assembly consists of the shuttle, two solid rocket boosters (SRBs), and an external fuel tank filled with liquid hydrogen and liquid oxygen. This fuel fires the three main engines located at the rear of the shuttle. To give the shuttle enough speed to escape the earth's gravity, the main engines are assisted by the two solid rocket boosters. Each of them is packed with over one million pounds of explosive powders.

Approximately two minutes into the flight, when the shuttle is about twenty-five miles above the earth, the SRBs automatically detach from the shuttle and parachute back to the earth. At this altitude, the shuttle's three main engines have enough power to propel the spacecraft to a speed of seventeen thousand miles per hour. These engines burn up the entire 1.5 million pounds of liquid hydrogen and liquid oxygen by the time the shuttle reaches an altitude of about 120 miles. When the external fuel tank is empty, it is also detached and falls to the earth.

Without fuel, the main engines shut down. Then the shuttle uses its small jet engines, known as the orbital maneuvering system (OMS), to maneuver in and out of orbit or to change orbits. To return to earth, the pilot uses the OMS to slow the shuttle down. As soon as it slows down even slightly, the shuttle begins to drop out of orbit and descend toward the earth.

Still traveling more than fifteen thousand miles per hour, the shuttle creates a tremendous amount of friction as it reenters the earth's atmosphere. The pilot must angle the craft just right to reduce the friction as much as possible, but it still reaches a temperature of 2,750° F. The twenty-five thousand heat shields covering the shuttle are all that prevent the craft from burning up.

The pilot's last maneuver is the most critical. A pilot uses the small jet engines to position the shuttle for a landing. These engines are shut down and the pilot brings the craft in for a landing traveling about two hundred miles per hour. Taking speed and wind into consideration, the pilot approaches the runway just right the first time because the shuttle has no power to fly by the landing site and come back for a second try.

Pictured below is the space shuttle *Atlantis* landing at Edwards Air Force Base.

Air Force Base in Southern California, the maiden voyage of the *Columbia* was nearly flawless. It had launched as a rocket, orbited the earth as a spacecraft, and landed as a glider. Bob Crippen, the pilot on this first space shuttle flight, remarked, "From a pilot's standpoint, you could not ask for a more superb flying machine."

On *Columbia*'s fifth flight, it carried a commercial communication satellite. In April 1983, the *Challenger*, the second vehicle in the shuttle fleet, successfully launched two more commercial satellites.

Over the next two years, the shuttle program continued to make significant gains. On several flights, the shuttle carried the portable *Spacelab*, a facility that allowed the crew to conduct the most complex scientific experimentation ever done in space. The *Spacelab* was a versatile laboratory in space. Working in shirtsleeve comfort, scientists in the *Spacelab* conducted research in astronomy, chemistry, biology, and other fields of science. Because of advances in computer technology, *Spacelab* could store hundreds of times more data than the *Skylab* space station of the early 1970s could.

Behind Schedule

In spite of the shuttle's advances, most members of Congress and the U.S. military were disappointed that the shuttle program remained behind schedule. Congress was anxious to see the shuttle start paying for itself, while the Air Force wanted to start launching more spy satellites and testing its strategic defense weapons. In July 1985, Congress sent NASA a strong signal that it would have to begin supporting itself soon. It cut the 1986 budget for the shuttle program by 5 percent.

Claiming that U.S. defense was too critical to rely on the uncertainties of the shuttle's flight schedule, the Air Force requested funds from Congress for its own space program. It planned to use expendable booster rockets to launch military satellites. Since the military was supposed to be one of the shuttle's primary customers, NASA could not afford to lose its business. Believing that meeting a tight schedule would force the Air Force to abandon its plan, NASA Administrator James Beggs announced in March 1985 that NASA would try to launch one shuttle flight per month. Calling this goal the shuttle's "flight manifest," Beggs stressed how important it was to the survival of the shuttle program:

> The next eighteen months are very critical for the shuttle. If we are going to prove our mettle and demonstrate our capability, we have got to fly out that manifest.

Despite all their efforts, NASA was able to launch only six shuttle flights in all of 1985. The 1986 schedule was revised to a more "realistic" goal of fifteen flights. Even to meet this goal, NASA would have to improve its turnaround time between flights. The plan was to maintain a regular cycle of launches, landings, booster recoveries, repairs,

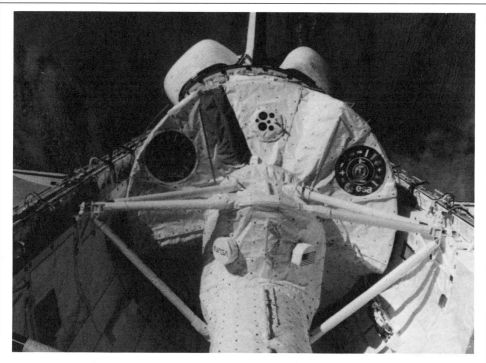

SPACELAB

The shuttle's large cargo bay allows it to carry bigger payloads, or cargo, with more unusual shapes than those launched by conventional rockets. One of its most unusual and most promising payloads is the *Spacelab*. It was designed as a cooperative effort between NASA and the European Space Agency. The *Spacelab* remains inside the cargo bay throughout the shuttle's flight. It lets scientists work in shirtsleeve comfort performing experiments in chemistry, biology, physics, medicine, astronomy, and other fields.

The *Spacelab* is composed of two modules. The workstation module is a cylinder-shaped pressurized cabin equipped with computers and work areas for up to six scientists. The second module is a U-shaped platform that can be equipped with telescopes, antennas, sensors, or other equipment to support the experiments being performed.

In the *Spacelab's* weightless environment, scientists on three different shuttle missions made ground-breaking progress in a number of fields. In chemistry, the absence of gravity makes it possible to mix materials much more thoroughly because heavier materials do not always sink to the bottom of the mixture. This has allowed researchers in the *Spacelab* to experiment with super-strength lightweight alloys, such as those composed of zinc and aluminum or lead and zinc.

In medical research, *Spacelab* scientists have separated cells of human blood with a purity far superior to any similar blood separations done on earth. This research could lead to products for the treatment of anemia, cancer, diabetes, glandular irregularities, and scores of other health problems. Future *Spacelab* missions on board the shuttle will take these ground-breaking efforts further and will undoubtedly lead to new discoveries.

Pictured above is *Spacelab* taken from the cargo bay of the space shuttle *Columbia*. The docking tunnel is in the foreground.

Astronauts complete an inspection of the heat tiles on the space shuttle *Columbia*.

and preparations for the next launch, much like a well-run airline.

Unfortunately, the shuttle was far more complex than any airplane. For one thing, it could be launched only in ideal weather conditions. For another, the only shuttle landing strip is on the West Coast and the only launchpads are on the East Coast. The shuttle has to be transported across country atop a B-52 after every flight. Before it could be launched again, it had to undergo extensive repairs and service.

After a shuttle returned to earth, heat tiles were often damaged or had fallen off completely. Technicians would find the steering and

braking systems well-worn after every flight. The extraordinary demand on the shuttle's high-pressure main engines would burn out hydraulic pumps much faster than had been expected. These repairs were far more extensive than the ones an airplane must undergo after each flight.

To further complicate matters, NASA did not really have a fleet of four complete shuttles. Because its budget was so tight, NASA did not have a large inventory of spare parts. Often, when a part broke or wore out on one shuttle, a replacement was "borrowed" from another shuttle. This practice became so common that whenever a shuttle landed at Edwards Air Force Base in California, it was immediately stripped of needed parts, from steering mechanisms to general-purpose computers. These were flown to Cape Canaveral and installed on the next scheduled shuttle. Although the turnaround times were nearly impossible to meet, Administrator Beggs remained determined to show the world that the shuttle was becoming increasingly reliable and economically feasible.

Careless Mistakes

This pressure to keep the shuttles flying meant that many NASA employees were overworked and sometimes made careless mistakes. These just set the flight manifest further behind schedule. In March 1985, for example, a heavy crane was dropped on the shuttle *Discovery*. It caused $200,000 worth of damage to the shuttle's cargo bay doors and delayed the next launch of the *Discovery* for two weeks.

Because of its complexity, a shuttle had to pass a rigorous series of inspections, called the flight readiness review, before each launch. In their review, NASA officials used a ranking method to indicate which parts of the shuttle system were most critical to flight safety. The most critical parts were ranked Criticality 1. This meant that if a Criticality 1 part failed to function correctly, it could endanger the lives of the crew.

Ideally, a spacecraft should have only a handful of Criticality 1 parts.

Most critical parts should have a ranking of 1-R. The *R* stands for redundancy. This means that if a part fails, a backup or another part automatically prevents a serious mishap. However, the shuttle was such a complex vehicle that inspectors continually reevaluated and updated the list of critical parts after each flight. During these reviews, they classified more and more parts to Criticality 1.

By the end of 1985, the shuttle system had more than seven hundred parts classified as Criticality 1. If any one of these parts failed, the vehicle could be destroyed. Before each launch, every item on the Criticality 1 list had to be certified as safe and operable by the appropriate NASA director.

One group of parts that had appeared on the Criticality 1 list for every shuttle flight since 1982 was the O-ring seal. This device sealed the joints connecting the four separate sections of the solid rocket boosters. These O-rings were made of synthetic rubber about one-fourth of an inch thick. They were designed by Morton-Thiokol, Inc., the builder of the solid rocket boosters, to prevent scorching hot gases from burning through the steel casing at the joints when the rockets were fired.

The O-ring seals were supposed to have a Criticality 1-R classification. This was because there were two O-rings in every joint. If gas leaked through the first, or primary, O-ring, the secondary O-ring

The two segments of the solid rocket booster are separated for inspection, to examine the O-ring seal.

was supposed to stop it before it burned through the casing.

After the second test flight of the *Columbia*, inspectors found that hot gas had burned through a few of the primary O-rings. Officials at the Marshall Space Center questioned Thiokol about the safety of the O-rings, but the builder of the SRBs repeatedly expressed confidence that the two-ring system was safe. Just to be sure, Marshall engineers conducted their own tests, and they obtained some rather disturbing findings.

They found that under the extremely high pressure of lift-off, the solid rocket boosters bulged so much that their joints shifted, or rotated. Because of this rotation,

Marshall engineers speculated that the secondary O-ring might not seal properly. If it did not seal, and if hot gas burned through the primary O-ring, it could pass through the joint and burn the outer casing of the booster rocket. This could cause the rocket to explode. Based on these tests, Marshall's shuttle project directors classified the O-rings as Criticality 1.

Over the next five years and twenty-five shuttle flights, inspectors continued to keep data on gas leaks, or "blow-by," at the solid rocket booster joints. In fifteen of these flights, they found evidence that hot gases had indeed blown by the primary O-ring.

Only once, however, had these

gases shown any evidence of also getting past the secondary O-ring. That was during the launch of *Discovery* Flight 51-C on January 24, 1985. At launch time the temperature at Cape Canaveral was fifty-three degrees Fahrenheit. A shuttle flight had never been launched in temperatures that low. After the SRBs from that launch had been recovered from the ocean, engineers at Marshall inspected all the O-rings. They found that the primary O-ring in the right booster's center joint had been burned so badly that the hot gases had also scorched the secondary O-ring. Fortunately, this ring had still sealed properly. In their report of this investigation, Marshall's engineers concluded that some erosion of the primary O-ring was normal.

Normal Wear and Tear

Although it continued to classify the O-rings as Criticality 1, Marshall treated the O-ring problem as normal wear and tear. It agreed with Thiokol that the two-ring system was safe. Just in case they were wrong about this, Marshall officials had instructed Thiokol to develop a system to assure that the secondary O-ring would seal properly. At the time that NASA managers began making preparations for *Challenger* Flight 51-L a year later,

however, no changes had been made to the O-ring assembly. But Thiokol had assured Marshall managers that "steps were being taken" to improve the sealing of the secondary O-ring.

In November 1985, just a month before Flight 51-L was scheduled to launch, NASA Administrator James Beggs resigned over accusations about unethical business practices. To replace Beggs, President Reagan appointed William Graham, an able administrator but one who had no previous experience in the space program. Graham informed William Lucas of the Marshall Space Flight Center and the other NASA space center directors that he was relying on them to carry out the Beggs flight manifest.

When the Marshall managers met for the flight readiness review of Flight 51-L in January 1986, they all knew how seriously their director, William Lucas, took the shuttle flight manifest. Lucas was determined that any delays in launching Flight 51-L would not be initiated by the people at Marshall.

Fortunately, the flight readiness review went without a hitch. The managers even decided to close their review of the O-rings, satisfied that they were safe. Along with Lucas, the managers were determined to "fly out that manifest."

Three

Waiting for a "Go"

The launch of *Challenger* Flight 51-L was originally scheduled for December 1985. When delays made that impossible, the flight was rescheduled for Friday, January 24, 1986, just two weeks after Flight 61-C of the *Columbia* space shuttle. In fact, while the *Columbia* was in orbit, the *Challenger* sat on launchpad B at Kennedy Space Center, awaiting final inspection and the arrival of a few "spare" parts from one of the other shuttles.

Aside from being the first flight of the Teacher in Space program, Flight 51-L would launch the TDRS-B satellite, the second of NASA's own Tracking Data and Relay Satellites. This satellite was capable of firing its own rockets to propel itself into an orbit twenty-three thousand miles above the earth's surface. From there, it would allow NASA to track and communicate with other in-flight shuttles and orbiting spacecraft.

Also in the *Challenger*'s cargo bay was the Spartan Halley Observatory, a photographic telescope. Once in orbit, the astronauts aboard the *Challenger* would use the shuttle's remote manipulator arm to release the observatory. It would then fly alongside the shuttle for twenty-two orbits, taking pictures of Halley's Comet, the famous comet with the fiery tail whose orbit took it past the earth once every seventy-six years.

NASA wanted Flight 51-L underway as soon as possible. This was because three other shuttle flights were scheduled after it that would need parts from the *Challenger*. These other flights were considered more important. Each one had an extremely narrow launch "window," the period in which a flight must be launched in order to accomplish its mission. If any of the three other flights were not launched on schedule, the launch would have to be delayed for months or even years until the earth and other planets were once again in the right positions. To make room for these more critical flights, Flight 51-L had to get off the launchpad before February 1 or be canceled indefinitely.

On January 23, after the final two months of training and a month of waiting at the Johnson Space Center in Houston, the *Challenger* crew arrived at Cape Canaveral. The next day high winds and a forecast of rain postponed the

The space shuttle *Challenger* lifts off on January 28, 1986.

launch. The crew anxiously awaited a new launch time in their quarters at the Operations and Checkout Building at Kennedy Space Center. For the crew members, the last few days had seemed like an eternity. Each of them had worked hard to prepare for his or her assignments on board the *Challenger*.

Throughout the eight days of the flight, mission commander Francis R. (Dick) Scobee would be responsible for seeing that all mission assignments were carried out according to plan. He would also maintain constant communication with Mission Control in Houston. Any decisions not covered in the mission plans rested with him.

His first mission in space, in 1984, had also been on the *Challenger*. During that flight Scobee served as pilot, and the crew rescued and repaired the *Solar Max* satellite. It was one of the shuttle program's most publicized successes, and it made Scobee something of a national hero. Ruggedly handsome, sincere, and plainspoken, he made an ideal publicity figure for NASA. After his first shuttle flight, he was frequently asked to give interviews or provide television commentary for other shuttle flights.

Sharing the flight deck with Commander Scobee would be pilot Mike Smith. Smith's most critical work would come at the end of the flight, when he would guide the *Challenger* out of its orbit and land it, like a huge glider, at Edwards Air Force Base in the Southern California desert.

Born in 1945, Smith was a graduate of the U.S. Naval Academy. He served in Vietnam as a flyer on an aircraft carrier, and after his tour of

The crew of *Challenger* mission 51-L. Pictured from left to right are: Christa McAuliffe, Gregory B. Jarvis, Judith Resnik, Francis R. Scobee, Ronald McNair, Michael J. Smith, and Ellison Onizuka.

duty there he became a test pilot for the Navy.

In 1980 Smith applied and was accepted to the astronaut training program in Houston.

Flight 51-L was to be his first trip into space. One woman, the mother of a high school friend, had told him he was crazy "for going up in that thing."

"Don't worry," he told her. "It's just as safe as getting in any other airplane and flying."

Confident of Shuttle's Safety

Judith Resnik was also confident of the shuttle's safety. On the upcoming *Challenger* flight, Resnik would operate the remote manipulator arm to release and retrieve the Spartan Halley Observatory. Resnik had helped perfect the design and operation of the shuttle's remote manipulator arm.

In 1966 she became one of the first women to receive a scholarship in engineering at the Carnegie Institute of Technology (now Carnegie-Mellon University) in Pittsburgh, Pennsylvania. After receiving her Ph.D. in biological engineering, Resnik applied for and received a place in the astronaut training program.

At NASA Judy applied her characteristic drive to excel. She ran and she lifted weights; in the months preceding her first shuttle flight in June 1984, she practically lived at the Johnson Space Center. Her stepmother, Betty Resnik, explains why Judy loved her work at NASA so much:

Any place that Judy had been before, she was always so much brighter than anyone else, in high school, in college. Until she got to NASA, people were always looking up to her. When she got there, though, there were all these intelligent people with the same interests. She had found what she called her family. They worked hard but they played hard. I think those had to be the happiest days of her life.

Working alongside Resnik on the *Challenger* would be physicist Ronald McNair, one of the first black men in space. His chief responsibility was observing Halley's Comet and interpreting the photographs taken by the Spartan Halley Observatory. McNair thought it was important to set an example for young blacks to follow. That is why he often flew to San Francisco, New Orleans, New York, and other parts of the country to address black students in colleges, high schools, and grammar schools.

One thing he told them was that anything is possible. As a child growing up in the rural town of Lakeside, South Carolina, during the 1950s and early 1960s, McNair had never imagined that he would one day become an astronaut. A black child in the segregated South was often told there were certain places blacks could not go and certain jobs they could not hold.

But no one could ever make Ron believe that he was not the smartest or the best at anything he tried. "Don't ever tell Ronald he can't do

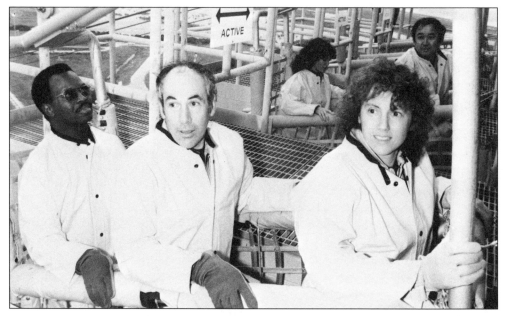

Five crew members of Flight 51-L during training operations. Pictured in the foreground are Christa McAuliffe, Gregory Jarvis, and Ronald McNair. In the rear are Ellison Onizuka and Judith Resnik.

something," McNair's father used to say. "I've tried and it doesn't work."

Another minority was also represented on the *Challenger* crew. As a member of the shuttle crew for Flight 51-C in January 1985, Ellison Onizuka had become the first Japanese-American in space and an overnight hero in the Japanese-American community and his home state. On Flight 51-L, Onizuka was in charge of deploying the TDRS-B satellite. Being an astronaut was something Onizuka had dreamed of ever since his childhood on the island of Hawaii.

In 1962, at the age of sixteen, Onizuka told his father and grandfather that he intended to become an astronaut. He told only one

other person of his dream: his Boy Scout leader Norman Sakata. Knowing Onizuka as well as he did, Sakata believed him. Years later, Sakata remembered his most famous Boy Scout: "He was cautious. He never made mistakes, this boy. He was the kind of person who wouldn't accept second best."

Before his first shuttle flight, Onizuka had put together a book containing insurance papers and letters for his wife and their two daughters, "just in case." Whenever he had mentioned the book to Lorna, it made her uneasy. So he did not mention the book before the *Challenger* flight. But he did something that Lorna later thought was rather strange. He told his daughters what he had written to them in the letters. And just before he left for Cape Canaveral, he had brought the book of insurance papers and important documents home from his office and left it where Lorna would be sure to find it. As always, Ellison Onizuka, the one time Eagle Scout, had been prepared.

Hardly prepared for his brief stint as an astronaut was forty-one-year-old Greg Jarvis. In fact, he was fond of telling people that his assignment to *Challenger* Flight 51-L was a "victory for the ordinary people." After he was selected as one of two engineers from Hughes Aircraft Company to ride the shuttle, he said, "You look at an astronaut who is just about a perfect human being, and here you are, your hair falling out, and they call you!"

Jarvis would have limited responsibilities. NASA had granted Hughes Aircraft Company two crew member positions, one for 1985 and another in 1986. It was NASA's way of rewarding Hughes's commitment to using the shuttle as the sole launch vehicle for their Leasat satellites. Since Jarvis was the manager in charge of the design of these satellites, he seemed to be an appropriate choice.

First Flight to Have Civilians

Challenger Flight 51-L was the first shuttle mission to have two civilians on board. The second was Christa McAuliffe, the highly publicized winner of President Reagan's Teacher in Space program.

McAuliffe first learned that she

Christa McAuliffe made history when she became the teacher selected to fly aboard the space shuttle.

had been chosen as the Teacher in Space on July 19, 1985. As she stood in the Roosevelt Room of the White House and clutched the small statue of a student and teacher gazing up at the stars, Sharon Christa McAuliffe choked back the tears and spoke into a sea of microphones:

> It's not often that a teacher is at a loss for words, I know my students wouldn't think so. I've made nine wonderful friends over the last two weeks. When that shuttle goes, there might be one body, but there's going to be ten souls I'm taking with me.

McAuliffe was a publicity dream for NASA. Thirty-six years old, of average height and build, with curly, medium-length, light brown hair, she was attractive, not beautiful. But when she smiled, her eyes sparkled with a genuine warmth and enthusiasm.

As a teacher, McAuliffe believed

that students learn about historic or current events best when challenged to experience them for themselves. She was constantly taking her students on field trips to courts, prisons, and city offices. She invited lawyers, congressmen, and judges to speak to her class. She assigned students to watch the stock market, to role play or reenact important events, and to keep journals of their daily lives.

This belief was something she intended to emphasize on her trip to space. When reporters asked her what she hoped to accomplish by being the first teacher in space, she replied:

> I would like to humanize the Space Age by giving a perspective from a non-astronaut, because I think the students will look at that and say, This is an ordinary person. This ordinary person is contributing to

history, and if they can make that connection then they're going to get excited about history, and they're going to get excited about the future. They're going to get excited about space.

Although she was the center of the media attention, McAuliffe remained mindful of her place in this mission. When this adventure was over, she intended to return to her home in Concord and resume her quiet life as a teacher and parent. Her career was not tied to the space program as the careers of the other six crew members were. She knew that their work in space was more vital than hers, and she worked and trained hard so that she would not seem a burden or need special assistance from them.

But by the time all seven of the *Challenger*'s crew members were quarantined at the Kennedy Space

Christa McAuliffe and backup teacher Barbara Morgan in training at Johnson Space Center.

Center in the final days before their flight, McAuliffe had earned the respect of the others. They recognized that she had worked to learn to maneuver in a weightless environment, to secure herself inside her emergency life-support pack, and to be in the right places at critical times so that she did not get in the way. At the same time, they saw that she took her role as NASA's link to the public seriously, sharing her experience and her observations in ways that would benefit the space program.

Late Friday afternoon, the crew received word that the launch had been rescheduled for Sunday, January 26, at 9:37 A.M. The night before the launch, both McAuliffe and Jarvis had trouble sleeping. So they slipped out of the astronauts' quarters (against regulations), found two bicycles, and rode around the space center. Except for a few lights burning in the nearby Operations Management Center, all was dark, cold, and very quiet. They could see the *Challenger* in the distance, poised on launchpad B. Everything seemed ready for the morning's launch. Like the other crew members, McAuliffe and Jarvis were completely unaware that NASA's managers had still not given the launch a final "go" or that frantic discussions and heated debates about the status of the launch would last long into the night.

Four

A Major Malfunction

On Monday morning, January 27, the seven-member crew boarded the *Challenger*. They were strapped in their seats, backs to the ground and feet pointing toward the sky, as the countdown ticked away second by second toward zero. At nine minutes before takeoff (T minus nine minutes), a flight mechanic discovered a faulty bolt on one of the shuttle's doors, and the countdown was stopped. Four hours later, with the astronauts still waiting in the same uncomfortable positions, the door was finally repaired. By then, however, the wind was blowing too hard to guarantee a safe launch. Flight 51-L had to be postponed again, until the next day, Tuesday, January 28.

Monday afternoon the temperature began to fall. Weather reports were forecasting record cold temperatures for Monday night. Allan MacDonald, the manager of Morton-Thiokol's solid rocket booster project, was in Florida for the launch. That evening he received a telephone call from the Thiokol plant in Utah. Several engineers there had heard the reports of freezing temperatures at the Cape. They expressed concern about the effect the cold weather might have on the solid rocket boosters' O-rings. MacDonald asked the engineers to collect their statistics on the performance of O-rings in cold weather and fax them to him.

MacDonald managed to arrange a telephone conference between the engineers at Thiokol and the Marshall representatives at Kennedy. Representing the Marshall Center were Stanley Reinartz, the shuttle project manager; Lawrence Mulloy, director of the solid rocket booster project; and George Hardy, deputy director of engineering.

Problems in Cool Weather

Before the conference began at 8:15 P.M., eastern standard time (EST), MacDonald made sure that Marshall's representatives had received the charts of data sent to him by the Thiokol engineers. These indicated that the most serious O-ring erosion and blow-by problems in previous flights had occurred when launches took place in cool weather. In fact, the worst blow-by had occurred at the coldest previous launch, which was fifty-three degrees Fahrenheit. The engineers from Thiokol unanimously

Main engine exhaust, solid rocket booster plume and an expanding ball of gas from the external fuel tank is visible after the *Challenger* accident.

recommended that a launch should not be attempted in temperatures below fifty-three degrees.

Mulloy, Hardy, and Reinartz could not believe what they were hearing. At least, they did not want to believe it. They knew that their director, William Lucas, would never accept Thiokol's last-minute data as proof that the O-rings would fail. Hardy announced that he was "appalled" by Thiokol's recommendation. Mulloy said angrily,

> My God, Thiokol, when do you want me to launch—next April? You guys are generating new launch commit criteria.

Reinartz requested that the engineers and managers at Thiokol reconsider their recommendation. If their final recommendation were still not to launch, he asked that they supply signed documentation with conclusive evidence that launching in cold weather would jeopardize the safety of the crew.

Opposed to Launch

At the Thiokol plant in Utah, the engineers asked for a few minutes to review their decision. After further discussion, they remained unanimously opposed to a launch in such cold temperatures. However, when Thiokol's Senior Vice-President Jerald Mason was told of his engineers' position, he called Robert Lund, the vice-president in charge of engineering, and several other top managers to his office. "Take off your engineering hat for a second and put on your management hat," he told Lund. Mason

wanted the engineers to reconsider in order to please the officials at the Marshall Space Center. Mason did not want to disagree with Marshall's managers, especially not at this late hour. He made it clear to Lund that the recommendation not to launch was not just the engineers' decision but a decision that might hurt the company's chance for future business with NASA.

After a thirty-minute discussion, the managers decided to overrule their engineers' recommendation. Thiokol Vice-President Joe Kilminster telephoned the Marshall representatives at Kennedy Space Center and gave them the news they were hoping to hear. Thiokol had changed its mind. It could not provide proof that launching the shuttle in this cold temperature would jeopardize the safety of the crew. Marshall's representatives asked Kilminster to fax them a signed report stating that conclusion.

When the report arrived, the Marshall representatives asked Allan MacDonald to sign it. MacDonald refused. He was one of the few managers at Thiokol who believed that the engineers' recommendation should have been heeded. But as far as the people at Marshall were concerned, the O-ring debate was over.

Meanwhile, the temperature continued to fall. At 1:30 A.M., launch director Gene Thomas ordered an inspection of the ice conditions on the launchpad. The inspection team reported that the ice conditions were the worst that they had ever seen. The scheduled launch time was moved from 9:38 A.M. to 11:00 A.M.

Tuesday morning at Cape Canaveral was cold but crystal clear, and the sun was beginning to warm the air. By the time Thomas ordered a second ice inspection at 8:30 A.M., the ice covering the launchpad and the icicles hanging from its rails were melting quickly. The ice team reported that conditions on the launchpad were looking more favorable for a launch. The National Space Transportation System Director Arnold Aldrich called a 9:00 A.M. meeting of the mission management team to discuss the pending launch.

Stanley Reinartz attended the meeting, but he did not mention his all-night ordeal with the Thiokol engineers. However, Robert Glaysher, a vice-president of orbiter operations at Rockwell, was also at the meeting. He conveyed the opinion of most Rockwell officials that the ice conditions made the launch unsafe. Their primary concern was that icicles hanging on the launchpad would fall and damage the heat tiles on the *Challenger*.

No One Seemed Alarmed

At 10:30 A.M., the ice team made its third inspection of the launchpad. No ice remained on the launchpad or on the shuttle itself. The team also reported that the surface temperature of the left solid rocket booster was thirty-three degrees Fahrenheit, while the right booster

Ice covered the platform on the fateful morning of the *Challenger* accident.

was only nineteen degrees. No one seemed alarmed by this report, even though the one rocket was thirty-four degrees colder than the temperature the engineers recommended. After receiving the report, the mission management team decided to go ahead with the launch.

At 10:35, a shiny silver van pulled up alongside the launchpad, and out stepped the five men and two women of the *Challenger* crew. Wearing their powder blue NASA jumpsuits, they strode to the mobile elevator that would transport them to the shuttle's flight deck. One of the launch technicians handed Christa McAuliffe an apple. Smiling, she handed it back to him and said, "Save it until I get back."

Obviously eager to get going, the crew climbed into the elevator.

Ice covers the launchpad before the *Challenger* takeoff. A shuttle launch had never been attempted under these conditions.

Once inside the shuttle, they put on their helmets and moved to their assigned positions. Seated up front on the flight deck were Commander Scobee and the pilot, Mike Smith. Behind them on the flight deck were Resnik and Onizuka. Seated in the mid-deck directly beneath the flight deck were McNair, Jarvis, and McAuliffe.

Outside the Launch Control Building, about three hundred yards from launchpad B, the VIP viewing grandstands were filled with excited spectators. Among them were fifteen third-graders from Concord, New Hampshire. They were all classmates of Christa McAuliffe's eight-year-old son, Scott. Grace and Ed Corrigan, McAuliffe's mother and father, were there, too, and so was her sister. Also on hand was Barbara Morgan, McAuliffe's alternate in the Teacher in Space program. The two had become close friends over the past year. A large party of Mike Smith's relatives and friends had made the drive from Beaufort, North Carolina, to see their hometown hero lift off.

The crew's immediate family members viewed the scene from the roof of the Launch Control Building. They stood shivering in the brisk morning air, nervous and proud. Cheryl McNair pushed her young son back and forth in his stroller. Steven McAuliffe held his arms around his two children. Scott, the older of the two, was shivering, but not just from the cold. Excitement shone unmistakably in

his sparkling brown eyes, just the way it always did in his mother's.

Lift-off!

The excitement mounted as the public address announcer continued to count down the seconds. After so many false starts, it looked like the real thing this time. "T minus one minute," the loudspeakers blared. In the grandstands all eyes turned toward the flight deck of the shuttle. At T minus six seconds, the *Challenger*'s three main engines began firing. Three seconds later, both solid rocket boosters ignited. "Two . . . one . . . lift-off!"

With the boosters roaring and pouring out billows of white smoke and great orange shafts of fire, the *Challenger* rose from the launchpad. All around them, the spectators felt the ground shake from the tremendous power of the booster rockets. They cheered, clapped, and screamed in approval.

At the moment of lift-off, flight control and communication with the crew switched from the Kennedy Space Center to Mission Control in Houston. Through the loudspeakers at Kennedy, the voices of the *Challenger* crew could be heard as they spoke with Mission Control:

T plus 0:07. Mission Control: Watch your roll, *Challenger*.

Scobee: Houston, *Challenger* roll program. [The first maneuver after lift-off is to rotate the shuttle so that it turns to face the earth.]

Mission Control: Roll program confirmed. *Challenger* now heading down range. Engines beginning to throttle down to 94 percent. . . . Will throttle down to 65 percent shortly. Velocity 2,257 feet per second [1,538 miles per hour]. Altitude 4.3 nautical miles. Three engines running normally. . . . Engines throttling up. Three engines now at 104 percent.

T plus 0:11. Smith: Go, you mother!

T plus 0:19. Smith: Looks like we've got a lot of wind up here today.

T plus 0:21. Scobee: Yeah. It's a little hard to see out my window here.

T plus 0:28. Smith: There's 10,000 feet [altitude] and Mach point five [1/2 times the speed of sound].

T plus 0:35. Scobee: Point nine.

T plus 0:40. Smith: There's Mach 1.

T plus 0:41. Scobee: Going through 19,000 feet.

T plus 0:43. Scobee: Okay we're throttling down.

T plus 0:57. Scobee: Throttling up.

T plus 0:58. Smith: Throttle up.

T plus 0:59. Scobee: Roger.

T plus 1:02. Smith: Thirty-five thousand. Going through 1.5.

T plus 1:05. Scobee: Reading 486 on mine [airspeed indicator].

T plus 1:07. Smith: Yep. That's what I've got, too.

Mission Control: Go at throttle up.

T plus 1:10. Scobee: Roger, go at throttle up.

T plus 1:13. Smith: Uhh . . . oh!

Seventy-three seconds into its flight, this was the last recorded word from the space shuttle *Challenger*. For a little more than one minute, viewers on the ground watched the *Challenger*'s beautiful

NASA technicians watch a shuttle liftoff at Mission Control in Houston.

Shocked spectators moments after the space shuttle *Challenger* explodes.

arching ascent as it roared into the sky. By then the orbiter was a white dot, seven miles above Cape Canaveral. Its white vapor trail was just beginning to diffuse when those on the ground saw an enormous white cloud suddenly form where the shuttle had been—a cloud filled with streaks of fire.

As they continued to watch, not at all certain what they were witnessing, a nightmare took form in the sky. The two booster rockets flew away from the great cloud of smoke, streaming off madly in opposite directions. Families of the crew watched in disbelief, still unable to comprehend what they were seeing. Beyond the cloud of darkening smoke, the sky filled with debris. Frantically, the spectators searched the sky for the orbiter, but it had vanished with the crew into a flaming ball of fire.

For thirty seconds that seemed like an eternity, the loudspeakers were silent. Then the somber voice of the Mission Control public address broke the silence:

> Flight controllers are looking very carefully at the situation. Obviously a major malfunction. We have no downwind. We have a report from the flight dynamics officer that the vehicle has exploded. The flight director confirms that. We are looking at all contingency operations, waiting for word of any recovery forces in the down-range field.

In the VIP grandstands, the stunned schoolchildren stared up at the adults with fear. Television cameras had been focusing on the faces of Grace and Ed Corrigan from the moment of lift-off. At first, they were both crying with joy.

Then, as the reality of what had happened began to register, the looks on their faces turned from joy to confusion to anguish. Mrs. Corrigan appeared to be repeating the words of the public address announcer to herself over and over, as if she could not believe what she had just seen and heard: "The vehicle has exploded. The vehicle has exploded."

Stunned Silence

On the roof of the Launch Control Building, one of Mike Smith's children cried, "I want you, Daddy. You promised nothing would happen." Hundreds of miles away, at McAuliffe's high school in New Hampshire, students had gathered in the school auditorium to watch the launch. They had brought party hats and noisemakers to celebrate the moment of lift-off. Now they sat in stunned silence, many still wearing their party hats, but their heads hung in disbelief.

A few minutes after the explosion, NASA officials gathered the crew's family members in the crew quarters. Ellison Onizuka's wife fainted. As she collapsed, her body brushed a light switch on the wall. For a moment, the room went black.

Fifteen minutes later, NASA official George Abbey met with the family members. "We don't know all the details," he said, "but it looks like there has been an explosion. I don't believe there is any hope for the crew."

The images of the explosion were played and replayed on television sets across the United States all day. For almost all Americans old enough to remember that day, these images of the *Challenger* soaring like an eagle one second and consumed in a ball of fire the next will always remain among their most vivid memories. For several minutes after the explosion, people remained confused about just what had happened.

Even after the public address announcer stated that the vehicle had exploded, the fact seemed to escape many of the onlookers. The children, especially, continued to shout excitedly as they felt the powerful aftershocks of the blast-off rumble through the ground. Slowly, as they looked up at the faces of the adults around them, they began to realize that something was terribly wrong.

NASA's spokespeople did little to eliminate the confusion. The agency implemented a temporary news blackout while it tried to sort out exactly what had happened. About five minutes after the explosion, the public address announcer at Mission Control said:

> At approximately a minute into the flight, there was an apparent explosion. The flight dynamics officer reported that the vehicle had exploded and impacted into the water. Recovery forces are proceeding to the area, including ships and C-130 aircraft. Flight controllers are reviewing their data here in Mission Control. We will provide you with more information as it becomes available.

That was to be the last public statement from NASA until a press conference was held five hours later. In the meantime, network television news commentators consulted experts and nonexperts alike for their reactions. For the first twenty or thirty minutes, they held out hope that somehow the crew had escaped. It was not common knowledge outside NASA that the shuttle did not contain a launch escape system.

Little Hope for Crew

Soon, however, it became clear that there was little hope for the crew. ABC News interviewed astronaut Gene Cernan by telephone. Cernan, from his office at Johnson Space Center, had viewed the accident on television. From what he had seen, he believed that "the crew members on board the shuttle did not have a prayer. With an explosion of that intensity, as fast as it happened, they would not have had time to activate an escape system if one had existed."

At 4:30 P.M., EST, NASA Associate Administrator Jesse Moore held a press conference. His voice trembled, as he told the American public what most of them had already assumed:

It is with deep, heartfelt sorrow that I address you here this afternoon. At 11:30 A.M. this morning, the space program experienced a national tragedy with the explosion of the space shuttle *Challenger* approximately a minute and a half after launch from here at the Kennedy Space Center.

I regret that I have to report that based on very preliminary search of the ocean where *Challenger* impacted this morning, these searches have not revealed any evidence that the crew of *Challenger* survived.

According to Moore, NASA still had no idea what had caused the explosion. None of the data from Launch Control or Mission Control had indicated anything out of the ordinary. Neither Moore nor anyone else from NASA mentioned any history of O-ring problems on the solid rocket boosters. Moore simply stated that a formal board would be established to thoroughly investigate the cause of the accident.

Few people were thinking about the cause of the accident that afternoon. Instead, the attention of the nation was focused on the tragic loss of seven men and women. Perhaps the brief public statement is-

President Ronald Reagan attempted to console a grieving nation after the shuttle explosion.

NASA officials, a military honor guard and escorts from the Astronaut Office are present at the shuttle landing facility as the remains of the *Challenger* crew are moved to Dover Air Force Base.

sued by Steven McAuliffe about his wife, Christa, expressed the emotion that many Americans felt: "We have all lost Christa."

President Ronald Reagan did what he could to keep that faith alive. As it happened, the president was supposed to be delivering his annual State of the Union address that evening. Instead, he postponed the address and spent the day reviewing the *Challenger* accident and helping the American people deal with the tragedy. In a televised speech that afternoon, he had special words for the families of the *Challenger* crew:

> Your loved ones were daring and brave, and they had that special grace, that special spirit that says, 'Give me a challenge and I'll meet

it with joy.' They had hunger to explore the universe and discover its truths. They wished to serve and they did—they served all of us.

Putting a teacher on the shuttle crew had been President Reagan's idea. At this time, he wanted to help comfort the schoolchildren—those who had watched the launch at Kennedy Space Center, those who were gathered in the auditorium at Concord High School, and others who watched the launch on television in classrooms across the country. These were his words to them:

> I know it's hard to understand that sometimes painful things like this happen. It's all part of the process of exploration and discovery, it's all part of taking a chance and expanding man's horizons. The fu-

ture doesn't belong to the faint-hearted. It belongs to the brave. The *Challenger* crew was pulling us into the future and we'll continue to follow them.

Finally, he addressed the general public with an inspirational memory of the crew:

> We will never forget them nor the last time we saw them this morning as they prepared for their journey and waved goodbye and 'slipped the surly bonds of earth to touch the face of God.'

On Friday, January 31, a memorial service for the seven crew members was held at the Johnson Space Center in Houston. It was attended by thousands of NASA employees, including the nation's entire corps of astronauts. Again it was President Reagan who assured the grieving families, the shaken NASA employees, and the American public that someday out of this tragedy would come a triumph:

> The sacrifice of your loved ones has stirred the soul of our nation, and through the pain, our hearts have been opened to a profound truth: the future is not free, the story of all human progress is one of a struggle against all odds. We learned again that this America was built by men and women like our seven star voyagers, who answered a call beyond duty, who gave more than was expected or required, and who gave it with little thought to worldly reward.

> Sometimes when we reach for the stars, we fall short. But we must pick ourselves up again and press on. . . . Today we promise Dick Scobee and his crew that their dream lives on. Man will continue his conquest of space, to reach out for new goals and ever greater achievements. That is the way we shall commemorate our seven *Challenger* heroes.

In the days immediately following the *Challenger* disaster, leaders of the space program repeatedly expressed their faith in the manned exploration of space. And most Americans kept their faith in the leaders of the space program. In the agonizing months that followed, however, the questions and investigations into the causes of the disaster would severely challenge that faith.

Five

The Long Road Back

Immediately after the accident, William Graham appointed an Interim Mishap Review Board to investigate the causes. Reviews of videotapes and of data gathered from Launch Control and Mission Control soon pointed the investigation toward the O-rings of the solid rocket boosters. When analyzed frame by frame, films of the launch clearly showed a puff of black smoke emerging from the right solid rocket booster just half a second after lift-off. Engineers detected the source of this smoke as the joint between the middle and lower sections of the right SRB. As the shuttle continued its ascent, smoke continued to pour out of this joint.

About one minute into the flight, the films first revealed a flame coming from the same joint. Second by second, the flame grew larger. Seventy-one and a half seconds into the launch, the right booster's gyroscope indicated that the nose of the rocket was swinging toward the external tank, while the lower part of the booster was swinging away from it. The flame from the right booster had burned through the steel bars that attached the lower end of the booster to the external fuel tank. As the lower end swung away from the external fuel tank, the nose of the booster crashed into the tank. It ruptured the wall inside the fuel tank that separated the liquid hydrogen from the liquid oxygen. As soon as these two combustible ingredients mixed in the presence of a flame, they caused an explosion so massive that the external fuel tank disintegrated and the shuttle broke into pieces.

In slow motion, the films also revealed something quite unexpected. Almost everyone believed that the shuttle had disintegrated in the explosion and the crew members had died instantly. But the films showed that a few seconds after the glowing fireball erupted, the crew compartment of the shuttle emerged from the cloud of smoke in one piece. Could the crew members possibly have survived the initial explosion? If so, were they locked inside a death trap because the shuttle had no escape system?

Immediately, submarines and surface vessels set out to search for the crew compartment. By early

Wreckage from the space shuttle *Challenger* mission is retrieved from the Atlantic Ocean by the U.S. Coast Guard and U.S. Navy vessels.

Large portions of the *Challenger*'s three main engines recovered from the Atlantic Ocean.

March they had recovered the crew compartment and almost half of the pieces of the *Challenger* from the ocean floor. The bodies of the astronauts were inside the crew compartment, still strapped in their seats. Medical experts worked for weeks trying to determine the cause of death, but their findings were inconclusive.

It is clear, however, that not all seven astronauts died from the initial explosion or even lost consciousness right away. Four of the seven emergency air packs on board were recovered. Three of the four had been used and two-thirds of their air supply exhausted. This meant that during the two and a half minutes it took the crew compartment to fall to the sea, at least three crew members were breathing. Also, one of the activated air packs belonged to Mike Smith, the pilot. Since it was mounted on the back of his seat, it could have been activated only by one of the other crew members, probably Ellison Onizuka, who was sitting directly behind Smith.

Even if the shuttle had been equipped with an escape system, most experts doubt that the crew could have reacted quickly enough to use it. Transcripts of the crew's communication with Mission Control show that the crew foresaw no sign of trouble until just three seconds before the explosion.

Could Not Have Survived

It is also doubtful that any of the crew members remained conscious for long after the explosion. If the explosion caused any air leaks at all in the walls of the crew compartment, then the compartment would have lost air pressure quickly. In that case, even with the emergency air packs, the crew members would have lost consciousness. At the moment the compartment struck the ocean, it was traveling about two hundred miles per hour. If any crew members were still alive at that time, they could not have survived the force of impact.

More disturbing, however, than the facts of how the accident oc-

curred or how the crew died, were the questions the investigation raised about why the accident happened in the first place. President Reagan decided that NASA's own review board could not answer these questions satisfactorily. He wanted an objective evaluation of NASA's own role in the disaster. On February 3, he created the Presidential Commission on the Space Shuttle *Challenger* Accident and appointed former secretary of state William Rogers to chair the eleven-member commission. Aside from Rogers, the commission was comprised of some of the country's leading experts in space exploration. They came from private business and from leading universities. Also on the commission were astronaut Sally Ride, who had been the first American woman in space, and Brig. Gen. Chuck Yeager, the retired test pilot who was the first pilot in the world to break the sound barrier. The goals of the Rogers Commission were to determine what had caused the accident, who was responsible for the accident, and how similar disasters could be avoided in the future.

For five months, the commissioners questioned key personnel at NASA and key employees of the shuttle's main contractors. Until the commission delivered its findings and recommendations, President Reagan ordered all shuttle flights suspended.

The evidence was overwhelming that the explosion had been caused

Inspecting the O-ring. Failure of the O-ring was determined to be a major cause of the *Challenger* disaster.

by the failure of the O-ring pressure seals in the joint between the middle and lower sections of the right solid rocket booster. As the prelaunch inspection had shown, the outer surface of this booster was only nineteen degrees Fahrenheit at launch time. Because the primary and secondary O-rings were so stiff from the cold, they were probably not flexible enough to form an airtight seal. Therefore, when the hot gases burned through the primary O-ring, the secondary ring was not in the proper position to stop the gases from burning right through the outer casing.

No Explanation

The Rogers Commission wanted to know why NASA had permitted the shuttle to fly when they knew about the O-ring problem and when the engineers who had designed these seals recommended against launching in such cold weather. Marshall Space Center Director William Lucas testified that his own engineers had concluded that the O-ring flaw was protected by the backup of a secondary O-ring. But when presented with evidence that even the secondary O-ring had shown signs of erosion on the coldest previous shuttle launch, Lucas did not have an explanation. And when asked whether he had ever reported the O-ring problem to Arnold Aldrich, director of the National Space Transportation System, the strong-willed Lucas replied, "I have never on any occasion reported to Mr. Aldrich."

A segment of the *Challenger*'s right wing after being recovered from the Atlantic Ocean.

Normally, Stanley Reinartz, shuttle project manager at Marshall, was responsible for reporting to Aldrich. Aldrich, in turn, was expected to report to Jesse Moore, the associate administrator of NASA. Neither Aldrich nor Moore had heard anything about the night-long arguments over O-rings between Thiokol engineers and the managers from the Marshall Space Center.

Under questioning by the Rogers Commission, Reinartz acknowledged that he had informed William Lucas, his director, of Thiokol's concerns. "But I did not perceive any clear requirement for interaction with Level 2," he said. When asked why not, Reinartz replied, "The concern was worked [out] with full agreement among all responsible parties." As evidence, Reinartz presented a document signed by Thiokol Vice-President Joe Kilminster the night before the accident. The document stated that Thiokol had no evidence to prove the O-rings were unsafe in cold temperatures.

Failure of NASA

The Rogers Commission submitted its final report to President Reagan on June 6, 1986. The report placed the responsibility for the shuttle accident squarely with NASA. The shuttle explosion was caused not only by the failure of a solid rocket booster joint but also by the failure of NASA "to understand and respond to facts obtained during testing." The commissioners concluded that even Level 1 authorities at NASA had received enough information about faulty O-rings by August 1985 that they should have ordered a discontinuation of shuttle flights until the problem had been solved.

The commission also found fault with NASA's chain of command. In its final report, it stated that "project managers felt more accountable to their center management than to the shuttle program." They were especially critical of William Lucas, director of the Marshall Space Center. His leadership had led "management at Marshall to contain potentially serious problems and to attempt to resolve them internally rather than communicate them forward." In other words, the managers were afraid to inform anyone that they had a problem, even when they knew they had one.

Some members of the Rogers Commission wanted the report to use even stronger language to condemn the inept management policies that had led to the fatal launch of the *Challenger*. One commissioner, former Nobel laureate Dr. Richard Feynman, felt so strongly about this that he added his personal commentary to the commission's final report. Feynman concluded that NASA officials altered the safety criteria so that flights could be certified on time:

> They therefore fly in a relatively unsafe condition with a chance of failure of the order of 1 percent. Official management claims to believe the probability of failure is a thousand times less.

The Rogers Commission called for a reevaluation of the chain of command within NASA. It claimed that the individual space centers, like Marshall in Huntsville, Johnson in Houston, Kennedy in Cape Canaveral, and others scattered throughout the country, were too independent. It recommended that NASA take immediate steps to make sure that all work related to the shuttle be subject to the approval of the NASA program manager.

The report also recommended the establishment of a new Level 1 position within NASA: an associate administrator of safety. Finally, the commission wanted to see greater representation by the astronauts in the decision-making process for manned space operations. It encouraged NASA to move former astronauts into management positions and to include crew commanders in all flight readiness reviews and mission management teams.

Perhaps the most far-reaching recommendation of the Rogers Commission was a call to reconsider the shuttle's mission and to establish a flight rate "consistent with its resources." It urged NASA to shift commercial payloads to expendable

William P. Rogers, chairman of the Presidential Commission on the Space Shuttle *Challenger,* listens to testimony.

rockets. The commission report stated that "the nation's reliance on the shuttle as its principal space launch capability created a relentless pressure on NASA to increase the flight rate."

One of the commission's most important recommendations was that the joints and O-rings on the shuttle rocket boosters be redesigned and thoroughly tested before another shuttle flight was flown. The commissioners also made specific recommendations to improve the shuttle's brakes, landing system, steering, and durability.

When the final report of the Rogers Commission was made public, along with Feynman's comments, it became clear that another shuttle would not fly for many months. Not only did engineers have to redesign critical elements of the shuttle and its launch boosters, but NASA itself had to be reorganized.

Problems Inside NASA

The *Challenger* disaster revealed problems inside NASA that had existed for years. Investigative reporters even found evidence that the *Challenger* may have been further doomed by the way NASA first selected the companies to build the shuttles.

In 1972, when those decisions were made, there were four chief competitors for the contract to build the shuttle vehicle. They were the Space Division of North American Rockwell, the Grumman Aerospace Company, Lockheed Missiles

---

A SAFER SHUTTLE

Besides improving the SRB joints, NASA made more than one hundred other safety improvements to the space shuttle. The most notable of these are listed below.

1. The steering system, which works by directing the air that strikes the nose of the shuttle, was made firmer, to keep the craft steady while landing in heavy crosswinds.

2. An escape system was added to allow astronauts to escape from a crippled shuttle. In case of emergency, astronauts will now be able to blast open an emergency exit on the left side of the crew compartment. As soon as the exit opens, a flexible chute will inflate, allowing the astronauts to slide clear of the wings and parachute to safety.

3. A safety latch was added to the main fuel valves to prevent accidental shutoff.

4. Thicker axles and more powerful brakes will make landings safer.

5. Stronger reinforcement of the wings will stabilize flight, especially during reentry and landing.

---

and Space Company, and McDonnell-Douglas Corporation's Astronautics Company.

Most industry leaders believed that Grumman held an edge over the competition. It had already worked closely with NASA in designing the launch system for the shuttle, consisting of the solid rocket boosters and external fuel tank. Grumman also had several past successes with NASA, including the design and construction of the Lunar Excursion Module driven by astronauts during Apollo missions.

McDonnell-Douglas also submitted a strong bid. Its proposal included an escape system that might protect the shuttle crew during the first two minutes of a launch, the most dangerous phase of a flight. Part of the escape system it proposed was an alarm that would sense hot gases leaking from the solid rocket boosters. If such a leak were detected, the alarm would automatically detach the booster rockets and activate the escape system.

Neither Grumman nor McDonnell-Douglas received the contract to build the shuttle. The contract was awarded to Rockwell. Rockwell's proposal did not include an escape system. NASA officials decided that it would have added too much extra weight. So the space shuttle became the first manned U.S. spacecraft without an escape system. Many ex-

perts believed this was a grave mistake. As Tom A. Brosz, the highly respected editor of *The Commercial Space Report*, commented:

> It is inconceivable that any competent designer of an aerospace flight system could create a vehicle which lacked the capability for safe abort during the most critical part of the launch.

Why was Rockwell selected instead of Grumman or McDonnell-Douglas? Many experts have speculated that it was for political reasons. The administrator of NASA during this time was James Fletcher. Fletcher's associate administrator for Manned Space Flight was Dale Myers, who had been the vice-president and manager of Rockwell's

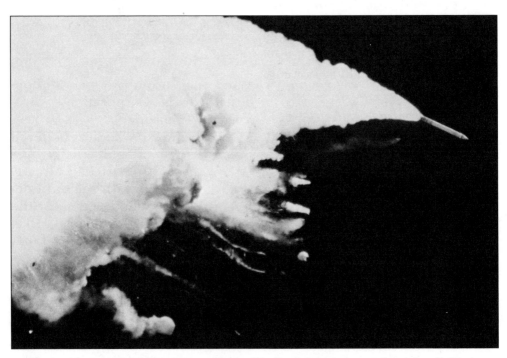

Debris emerges from the space shuttle *Challenger* moments after takeoff. Photos like these were used to determine the cause of the disaster.

Space Shuttle Development Division before joining NASA. In fact, in 1976 Myers left NASA and returned to Rockwell. Although no one has ever proven that Myers or Fletcher awarded the contract to Rockwell because of these connections, these two officials handpicked the members of the Source Evaluation Board that granted the major contract to Rockwell.

Questionable Contract Award

Perhaps the most questionable contract award of all was the choice of Morton-Thiokol to build the solid rocket boosters. In July 1973, NASA requested bids for the SRBs from three major companies: United Technologies, Aerojet Solid Propulsion Company, and Lockheed Propulsion Company. All three of these companies were based in California. It also requested a bid from Morton-Thiokol. At the time, Morton-Thiokol was a little-known company headquartered in Brigham City, Utah, the home state of NASA Administrator James Fletcher.

In most categories, the Source Evaluation Board gave Lockheed and Aerojet the highest scores. Lockheed scored higher in design and engineering, while Aerojet had the highest rating in the safety category. Its design called for a one-piece SRB instead of a multistage rocket. This design would have eliminated the need for O-rings altogether.

When James Fletcher announced that the contract for the SRBs had been awarded to Thiokol, it came as a surprise to almost everyone.

Could Fletcher have influenced the Source Evaluation Board's decision? The contract certainly provided jobs for thousands of citizens and added millions of dollars to the economy of his home state. Fletcher also had close ties with the U.S. senators from Utah, Wallace F. Bennett and Frank Moss. In 1971, when the Senate's Aeronautical and Space Sciences Committee endorsed Fletcher's nomination as NASA administrator, Frank Moss was the chairman of the committee. And Bennett testified before the committee that he had known Fletcher for twenty-five years. He described him as "one of the most able administrators in the state of Utah."

Suspecting foul play, the other competitors for the SRB contract protested NASA's choice of Thiokol. Following the normal procedure for such a protest, they appealed the decision to the federal Government Accounting Office (GAO). After reviewing the case, the GAO recommended to NASA that it reconsider its decision. However, the GAO could not prove that NASA's Source Evaluation Board had done anything illegal, so it could only recommend that the board reconsider its decision. After reconsidering, NASA still awarded the contract to Thiokol.

Ironically, after President Reagan received the report of the Rogers Commission on the *Challenger* accident, one of his first steps in reorganizing NASA was to reappoint

James Fletcher as the new NASA administrator. And one of Fletcher's first steps was to renew the contract with Morton-Thiokol to build solid rocket boosters with redesigned joints and O-rings.

Was NASA about to make the same mistakes over again, or could NASA benefit from the knowledge and experience of Fletcher and Morton-Thiokol? It may never be possible to make such a judgment, but both NASA and Thiokol began immediately to implement the recommendations of the Rogers Commission.

Changes at Morton-Thiokol appeared to assure a greater emphasis on safety and a greater voice for its engineers. Allan MacDonald and Roger Boisjoly, the two engineers who had been most vocal in urging NASA not to launch the *Challenger*, were assigned to head the company's redesign of the solid rocket booster.

Nearly three years passed before MacDonald and Boisjoly were satisfied that they had developed a safer joint and O-ring system. Besides improving the way the two ends of the joint fit together, they added a third O-ring seal to each joint. The new joint seems to accomplish what the old one never did—actual redundancy. In the meantime, the fleet of three shuttles underwent over one hundred other modifications to improve safety. Each of the shuttles was equipped with an emergency escape chute that may permit astronauts to escape from the shuttle if something goes wrong during the critical first two minutes of a launch. Landing and steering mechanisms, brakes, fuel valves, axles, and wing durability were improved.

Important Legacy

The most important legacy of the *Challenger* tragedy and the seven crew members who gave their lives to the U.S. space program may be a more intelligent, well-planned approach to future space efforts. National leaders began to view the shuttle program more realistically. Until it has proven 100 percent reliable over several years, only trained, professional astronauts will fly on shuttle missions. There will be no more teachers in space or politicians in space for many years to come.

Strangely, the *Challenger* accident led to stronger public support for space exploration. The American public, like NASA itself, needed to move on, to experience greater success in space. Without that, the loss of the *Challenger* crew would seem even more tragic and senseless.

On Thursday morning, October 6, 1988, thirty-two months after the *Challenger* disaster, the shuttle *Discovery* stood in an upright position on launchpad A at the Kennedy Space Center. On board, the shuttle's five astronauts strapped themselves in their seats. Led by Commander Fred Hauch, this was the most experienced crew NASA had ever put together for manned space flight. There were no teachers, no

FUTURE SHUTTLE MISSIONS

After the *Challenger* disaster, President Ronald Reagan ordered NASA to reevaluate the shuttle's place in the space program. As a result, the agency has developed specific goals for the shuttle and other manned space projects. The primary goal of the space shuttle will be to carry the people and supplies needed to build a permanently manned space station by 1995.

This orbiting station will be the hub of future U.S. space activities. It will have telescopes more powerful than the Hubble telescope, along with space-to-earth communications facilities and observatories for monitoring weather and other environmental conditions on earth. Eventually, additions to the space station will be made to house employees and equipment for manufacturing superior-quality medicines, alloys, optical lenses, and other products.

The space station will also be a base from which to launch probes into deep space. In 1990, President George Bush announced the goal of putting a human on Mars by July 2019, fifty years after the first humans set foot on the moon. In all of these endeavors, the space shuttle will be the freight and passenger line between the earth and the space station.

Pictured here is an artist's conception of the U.S. space station under development.

politicians, and no other civilians on board. Nevertheless, this crew had trained longer and harder than any previous shuttle crew.

At 10:00 A.M., a weak wind began to blow across the Cape. The mission management team reviewed engineers' analyses on what effect the wind might have on the coming launch. The engineers recommended proceeding with the launch, and the countdown continued. At 11:38 A.M., exactly the same time the *Challenger* had lifted off, the solid rocket boosters fired. As spectators in the VIP viewing grandstands looked on anxiously, it was hard for them not to relive the horror of the *Challenger*: the apparently perfect lift-off as the shuttle cleared the launch tower, into the graceful roll as it turned belly up to slice through the dense atmosphere, and then the ghastly, orange fireball and cloud of white smoke.

But two minutes into its flight, as the *Discovery* soared out of sight, the solid rocket boosters could be seen floating gently back to earth beneath their parachutes. The *Discovery* was on its way, and the United States was back in space.

The flight of the space shuttle *Discovery* helped to heal some deep wounds. For the moment, as message lights in Times Square flashed, "America Returns to Space," most Americans were glad to be back in space. To the five astronauts aboard the shuttle, there was no question that this was the right decision. As one of them said to Mission Control shortly after the *Discovery* entered its orbit,

> We sure appreciate you all gettin'
> us up into orbit, where we should
> be.

Glossary

abort: To end a mission early due to an emergency.

blow-by: The leaking of hot gases through a joint in a solid rocket booster.

cargo bay: The unpressurized area in the middle of the shuttle that holds satellites and other cargo.

downlink: Radio contact between Mission Control and a spacecraft.

expendable: Not reusable.

external fuel tank: The large cylindrical tank attached to the shuttle that supplies fuel to its main engines.

GAO: Government Accounting Office; office responsible for overseeing federal government spending.

gyroscope: An instrument used in navigation and aviation to measure how level something is.

hydraulic pump: A pump that works by the force of a moving liquid.

malfunction: The failure of something to work as it should.

Mission Control: The department of NASA that communicates with and gives instructions to the crew members of a spacecraft after it has been launched.

mission specialist: A shuttle crew member responsible for conducting experiments and looking after the cargo.

NASA: National Aeronautics and Space Administration; agency in charge of all U.S. space exploration.

news blackout: A period in which no news about a particular incident is made public.

orbit: The path of a natural or an artificial body revolving around a larger body, such as the path of a planet going around the sun.

O-ring seal: A synthetic rubber ring used to seal the joints in the solid rocket boosters.

payload: The cargo carried in the cargo bay of the orbiter.

prototype: An original model made for testing before making others like it.

quarantine: To place in isolation and restrict visitors.

reentry: Return to the earth's atmosphere.

satellite: An artificial object put into orbit around the earth.

scrub: To cancel a launch after the final countdown has begun.

solid rocket booster: A rocket that uses explosive powder for fuel. It is usually used to help lift a spacecraft off the ground.

STS: Space Transport System; the shuttle program.

supersonic: Faster than the speed of sound.

Suggestions for Further Reading

Allaway, Howard, *The Space Shuttle at Work*. Washington, DC: NASA, 1979.

Barrett, N.S., *Space Shuttle*. New York: Franklin Watts, 1985.

Bendick, Jeanne, *The First Book of Space Travel*. New York: Franklin Watts, 1985.

Billings, Charlene, *Christa McAuliffe: Pioneer Space Teacher*. Hillside, NJ: Enslow Publishers, 1986.

Billings, Charlene, *Space Station: Bold New Step Beyond Earth*. New York: Dodd Mead, 1986.

Cross, Wilbur, *Space Shuttle*. Chicago: Children's Press, 1985.

Stern, Alan, *The U.S. Space Program After Challenger*. New York: Franklin Watts, 1987.

Works Consulted

DeWaard, E. John, *History of NASA: America's Voyage to the Stars*. New York: C.N. Potter, 1988.

Fichter, George S., *The Space Shuttle*. New York: Franklin Watts, 1981.

Hohler, Robert T., *"I Touch the Future": The Story of Christa McAuliffe*. New York: Random House, 1986.

Lewis, Richard S., *Challenger: The Final Voyage*. New York: Columbia University Press, 1988.

McConnell, Malcolm, *Challenger: A Major Malfunction*. Garden City, NY: Doubleday, 1987.

Newsweek, "After the Challenger," October 10, 1988. pp. 25-38.

Science, "Commission Finds Flaws in NASA Decision-Making," March 14, 1986. pp. 1237-1238.

Shayler, David, *Shuttle Challenger*. New York: Prentice Hall, 1987.

Smith, Melvyn, *Space Shuttle: U.S. Winged Spacecraft: X-15 to Orbiter*. Somerset, England: Haynes Publishing Group, 1985.

Torres, George, *Space Shuttle: A Quantum Leap*. Novato, CA: Presidio Press, 1986.

Trento, Joseph, *Prescription for Disaster*. New York: Crown, 1987.

The Washington Post, "Challengers: The Inspiring Life Stories of the Seven Brave Astronauts of Shuttle Mission 51-L," New York: Pocket Books, 1986.

Index

About the Author

The Author, Timothy Levi Biel, was born and raised in eastern Montana. A graduate of Rocky Mountain College, he received a Ph.D. in literary studies from Washington State University.

He is the author of numerous nonfiction books, many of which are part of the highly acclaimed Zoobooks series for young readers. In addition, he has written *The Black Death: World Disasters*.

Picture Credits